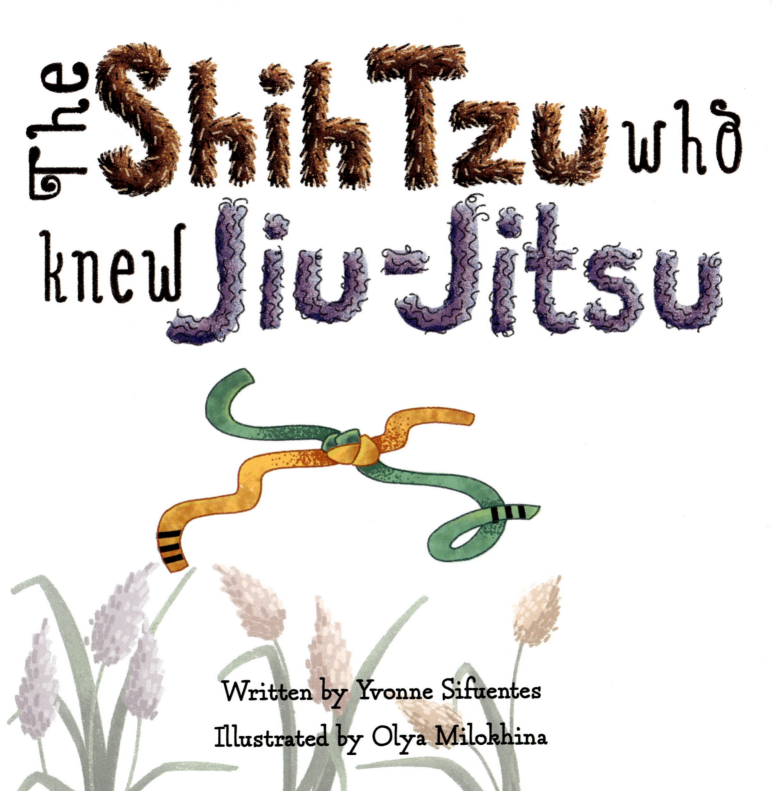

To all of the instructors who passionately teach children the essential principles of
jiu-jitsu.
It's one thing to teach a dog new tricks.
It's yet another to show him the way.

Confidence
It's what lets you stand tall.
Jiu-jitsu
It's the foundation upon which you stand.

A Publication of:
Soft Paw Press
P.O. Box 443
McQueeney, Texas 78123

The Shih Tzu Who Knew Jiu-Jitsu
Copyright © 2018 by Yvonne Sifuentes All rights reserved.
First Edition
ISBN-13: 9781732520905
Library of Congress Control Number: 2018907655
Children's Fiction

All rights reserved. No part of this publication may be reproduced, stored in a retrieval system, or transmitted in any form or by any means, electronic, or otherwise, without the prior written permission of the copyright holder.

"In loving memory of my granny Lydia"
Olya M.

Like all Shih Tzus, Leo loved the outdoors. One day, as he was walking through his favorite park, he came face-to-face with a large pack of dogs who were notorious for causing trouble.

Leo was frightened. All he wanted to do was go home, but the sight of the dogs gave him chills.
He could barely move a muscle.

"What's your name, Short-Stack?" said a fierce-looking Rottweiler, towering over Leo.
His name was Weiler, and he was the pack leader.
"I'm Leo," he said nervously.
"Well, I've got news for you." said Weiler. "We're The Ruffs, and this is *our* turf. We decide who can be here."
"But it's a public park, and it's my favorite place to play." said Leo.

Weiler immediately advanced on Leo, and pinned him to the ground. Then, narrowing his eyes and baring his sharp teeth, he growled, "This is The Ruffs' park! Understand?"

Leo cowered beneath the Rottweiler, covering his face with his paws. A few moments passed before Weiler let out a nasty laugh, then released him.

"I'm just kidding," he said. "You should've seen your face! I tell you what, why don't you join our gang and hang with us?"

Leo didn't know how to respond. He was scared to say no, but knew that joining The Ruffs wasn't a good idea. Trembling with fear, he gulped, then said, "No, I don't want to be in a gang."

"Oh!" Weiler snickered. "You thought I was **asking** you ... well, you thought wrong. I'm *telling* you to join us." The rest of The Ruffs surrounded Leo threateningly, all of them looking down at the little dog.

"I'll let you go this time," said Weiler.
"But, if we see each other again, understand this... I will make you join the gang. Now run off!"

When Leo returned home, he wasn't his normal, cheerful self. The Ruffs had given him a choice: either join the gang, or never visit his favorite park again. "What should I do?" he whined loudly. "I love the park, but I can't face those dogs again."

Startling Leo, a voice nearby barked at him:
"Hey, you over there! What are you whimpering about?"

Leo peeked through his fence into the neighbor's yard, and noticed a dog house.

"Stop crying!" continued the voice.

"I'm not crying."

"Well, pretty close to it. Tell me what's wrong and maybe I can help you."

"Really?" asked Leo doubtfully.

A female poodle appeared at the entrance of the dog house.
"Who are you?" asked Leo. "I've never seen you around before."
"My name is Bon Bon," said the poodle. "I just moved here last night."

Leo giggled. "What's so funny?" exclaimed Bon Bon.

"Oh, nothing," replied Leo.

"I'd pictured someone else helping me out. It's just that I have a BIG problem, and I'm going to need someone a lot *bigger* than you to help me."

Bon Bon smiled and said, "Don't be fooled by my size. Looks can be deceiving. I tell you what... see that old wood pile in the back? Well, there's a hole in the fence there. Come over to my yard, then tell me all about it.

Leo made his way through the fence, then joined Bon Bon.
"It was a gang of dogs. They call themselves The Ruffs."
The poodle laughed. "The Ruffs? Are they up to no good again?"
"You know them?" asked Leo.
"Who doesn't know them? I've lived all over this town. Everyone knows The Ruffs." said Bon Bon.

"Well, it was my first time meeting them." He told Bon Bon what had happened at the park, especially about how frightened he was when he refused Weiler's demand.
"So, now that you know the whole story, do you *really* think you can help me?"

"Of course I can help you." answered Bon Bon. "But let me ask you something: have you ever heard of jiu-jitsu?"

"Jeewy what?" asked Leo, confused.

The poodle corrected him: "It's pronounced *joo-jit-sue*."

"No, I've never heard of jeewy-jit-sue," said Leo.

"It's a gentle art of self-defense that teaches you how to protect yourself. Let me explain ..."

Bon Bon trotted into her dog house and rummaged around for a few minutes. She then reappeared, wearing a robe-like outfit.

"What's that?" asked Leo.
"It's a *gi*," said Bon Bon.
"It's worn by those who train in jiu-jitsu. Now listen carefully. If you ever get into a situation where you have to defend yourself, there are four rules to remember:"

"Rule # 1: If you can, avoid fighting at all costs."

"Rule # 2: If you get attacked, defend yourself."

"Rule # 3: You should never kick or punch an attacker. Instead, try to restrain him or her and talk it out."

"But how do I do that?" asked Leo.

"When someone attacks you," explained Bon Bon, "protect your face, move forward like a rhino, grab him tightly, and take him to the ground."

As Bon Bon demonstrated the self-defense moves, Leo noticed how much control the poodle had over him. No matter how hard he tried, Leo could not free himself.

"Now, rule #4 is very important, so pay attention," said Bon Bon. "In jiu-jitsu, when you force your attacker to give up, it's called a *submission*."

"That hurts!" yelped Leo.
"Well, of course it hurts," replied Bon Bon.
"That's why it's the most important rule. Before applying these moves, you have to *talk* to the attacker so that you can give him a chance to leave you alone."

"Oh, I see," said Leo. "Jiu-jitsu seems great! But do you really think it could help someone as small as I am?"

Bon Bon laughed. "Do you realize you're talking to a poodle? I'm not exactly big by any means. Now come on, let's start practicing."

As the weeks passed, Leo's confidence began to grow and he became joyful again. He had learned so much about self-defense that the thought of The Ruffs didn't scare him anymore.

Finally, the day came when he decided to visit the park again. And who did he see first?
The Ruffs.
"Well, well, well," said Weiler. "Look who we have here. It's our old friend, Short-Stack."

Leo didn't want any trouble, but as he tried to walk away, The Ruffs surrounded him. There was no escape.
"I've been looking for you!
Are you ready to join us?" said Weiler.
Leo wasn't afraid. Remembering the four rules of jiu-jitsu, he looked at the Rottweiler straight in the eyes.
"No!" said Leo confidently. "You're not a good dog, and I don't want to be a part of your gang."

"What?" growled Weiler. "Nobody says no to me! I run this turf, so you will do as I say!"
Then, without warning, Weiler charged toward Leo.

Leo quickly protected his face and made a move that caught Weiler completely off-guard. The big dog struggled to break free as Leo held on to him tightly.

"What are you doing?" yelled Weiler. "Get off me!"
"Are you going to stop?" asked Leo. "There's no need for this."
"I don't negotiate with anyone," said Weiler, still struggling. "Especially not with someone as small as you!"
"Well then," said Leo, "you leave me no choice."
Leo applied a submission just like Bon Bon had taught him, forcing Weiler to cry out: "Okay, okay, I'll stop!"

The Ruffs couldn't believe their eyes. Their fearless leader had been defeated. "I don't understand," said a stunned Weiler. "It happened so fast, and you didn't even hit me! How is this possible?"

Leo stepped back and helped the big dog to his feet. Smiling, he replied, "Weiler, welcome to the art of jiu-jitsu."

As the rest of the gang looked on, Weiler spoke two words that no one had ever heard him say before: "I'm sorry." Leo looked straight into Weiler's eyes and said, "Do me a favor...stop being a bully. Treat others the way you'd like to be treated."

From that moment on, Weiler and The Ruffs had a change of heart. They wanted to learn from Leo and become better dogs. They asked him if he could teach them jiu-jitsu.

Leo was happy to show them what he'd learned from Bon Bon. He taught them the principles of jiu-jitsu, when to use them, and how to apply them in a confrontation.

The dogs soon became best of friends as they spent their days practicing jiu-jitsu and playing together in the park.

From then on, brave little Leo was forever known as the Shih Tzu who knew jiu-jitsu.

I would like to acknowledge...

My wonderful illustrator and friend, Olya Milokhina, for partnering with me on this book and taking on the challenge. This was an amazing journey and I know we will continue to work together on future projects.

My friend, mentor, editor and creative guide, Ros Hill. This book would not be possible if it wasn't for his direction. He is an author and illustrator from San Marcos, TX. You can check out his work at www.hillustrations.com.

My family for supporting me through this process, including my nieces and nephews who have been eagerly awaiting this book.

To the love of my life, Valentine De La Garza. Thanks to his countless hours of support and showing me how to promote my book, Leo and The Ruffs are now to be enjoyed by many.

My McQueeney family who believed in me and couldn't wait to see this book come to fruition.

My friends from the Gracie Jiu-Jitsu training center in New Braunfels, TX. It is there where my journey began and I wouldn't be where I am now if it weren't for them. A special thanks to my head instructor Everett Holmes who continues to model and teach us the principles of jiu-jitsu.

Finally, I would like to thank everyone - including those as far as Australia - who took part in supporting this book. You have spread the word and have helped this book become a reality. Thank you!

For more information about "The Rules of Engagement" and how to make your child "Bullyproof", please visit www.gracieuniversity.com.

Made in the USA
Las Vegas, NV
06 January 2022